Acknowledgement of Land & of the Traditional Owners of this Land

I would like to acknowledge the Gadigal people of the Eora Nation, upon whose stolen land I stand on today.
I recognise that this land was never terra nullius — the land belonging to these peoples was never ceded, given up, bought or sold.
I would like to pay my respects to Aboriginal Elders past, present and emerging, and I extend this acknowledgement to all Aboriginal and Torres Strait Islander people.

Children of the Revolution

Well, you can bump and grind, it is good for your mind
Well, you can twist and shout, let it all hang out

But you won't fool the children of the revolution
No, you won't fool the children of the revolution, no no no

Well, you can tear a plane in the falling rain
I drive a Rolls Royce 'cause it's good for my voice

But you won't fool the children of the revolution
No, you won't fool the children of the revolution, no no no, yeah

But you won't fool the children of the revolution
No, you won't fool the children of the revolution

No, you won't fool the children of the revolution
No, you won't fool the children of the revolution, no way, yeah, wow

-Marc Bolan

CONTENTS

1: If They LO♥E You...
(Se ti Amano...)
2: State of Flux
(Stato di Flusso)
3: I'm in Training
(Sono in Allenamento)
4: It Feels So Real
(Sembra Così Reale)
5: Just Because We're Not Friends
(Solo Perché non Siamo Amici)
6: Surround Yourself with Those That Have Talent
(Circondati di Persone che hanno Talento)
7: LO♥E Me conditionless
(Amami Senza Condizioni)
8: Living in a Delusion
(Vivere in un'Illusione)
9: I Am NOT Needy!
(NON Sono Bisognoso!)
10: Lost in a Lost World
(Perso in un Mondo Perduto)
11: The Last Person Standing
(L'ultima Persona in Piedi)
12: You Were Right
(Avevi Ragione)
13: I'm a Spirit Trapped on this Planet
(Sono uno Spirito Intrappolato su Questo Pianeta)
14: Thestory
(Lastoria)
15: My Home is Aways Open
(La Mia Casa è Sempre Aperta)
16: "da Boyz"
("i Ragazzi")
17: Do Not Express Yourself
(Non Esprimerti)

CONTENTS

18: Who the FUCK are You?
(Chi CAZZO Sei?)
19: Like a Rolling Stone
(Come una Pietra Rotolante)
20: Tough Guys Don't Dance
(I Duri non Ballano)
21: I Wish I Was You
(Vorrei Essere Te)
22: I Am SO SORRY I FUCKED Up Our Friendship
(Mi Dispiace Tanto di aver Rovinato la Nostra Amicizia)
23: Killer on the Road
(Assassino sulla Strada)
24: I Don't LO♥E You Anymore
(Non Ti AMO Piu')
25: I Bring You LIFE
(Ti Porto la VITA)
26: Sei Forte
(You are Strong)
27: I Don't Want to Let You Go
(Non Voglio Lasciarti Andare)
28: There is No One!
(Non C'è Nessuno!)
29: No Expectations
(Senza Aspettative)
30: LO♥E in Vain
(Amore in Vano)
31: Sweet Vagina
(Dolce Vagina)
32: Don't Chase It
(Non Inseguirlo)
33: Psychopath or Sociopath?
(Psicopatico o Sociopatico)
34: My Delusion/Your Reality
(La Mia Illusione/La Tua Realtà)

CONTENTS

35: No PRESSURE
(Nessuna Pressione)
36: In "Absentia"
(Nella Assenza)
37: Any LO♥IN' is Good LO♥IN'
(Ogni AMORE è un Buon AMORE)
38: You're a Fantasist
(Sei un Fantasista)
39: Mr Rejection
(Signore Rifiuto)
40: Do Not Expect Anything
(Non Aspettarti Nulla)
41: Don't Beg For LO♥E!
(Non Implorare AMORE!)
42: Virus
(Virus)
43: State of Mind
(Stato Mentale)
44: Paradise
(Paradiso)
45: The Stranger
(Lo Sconosciuto)
46: Life Rules
(The Rules of Life)
(Le Regole della Vita)
47: By the Rivers of Babylon
(Presso i Fiumi di Babilonia)
48: Can We Start Again?
(Possiamo Ricominciare?)
49: Epiphany
(Epifania)
50: In the Garden of Eden
(Nel Giardino dell'Eden)

If They LO♥E You...

(Se ti Amano...)

If they LO♥E you...
...you don't have to do a thing!

"The Don"
16.01.2023

STATE OF FLUX

(Stato di Flusso)

Everything is *changing*.
Everything is *unstable*.
Everything is in *motion*.
Everything is in *dynamics*.
Everything is *fluidic*.
Everything is in *turmoil*.
Everything is *out of control*.
Everything is in *chaos*.
Everything is in a *"State of FLUX"*!

"The Don"
16.01.2023

I'm in Training

(Sono in Allenamento)

I'm in training.
What for you may ask?
I'm in training for *life*.
I'm in training for *living*.
I'm in training for *DEATH!*

What are you in training for?

"The Don"
17.01.2023

It Feels So Real

(Sembra Così Reale)

It feels so real but it's *so fake...*
...that's LO❤E.

"The Don"
17.01.2023

Just Because We're Not Friends
(Solo Perché non Siamo Amici)

Just because we're not friends anymore doesn't mean I don't care about you!

"The Don"
19.01.2023

SURROUND YOURSELF WITH THOSE THAT HAVE TALENT
(Circondati di Persone che hanno Talento)

They will make you SHINE!

"The Don"
19.01.2023

LO♥E Me conditionless

(Amami Senza Condizioni)

With absolutely NO conditions!
Is that possible?
Is it EVEN conceivable!
To LO♥E conditionless!

"The Don"
19.01.203

Living in a Delusion

(Vivere in un'Illusione)

I prefer to live in a delusion.
What is the alternative?
A world without delusions?
A delusionless world?
That is the world I am trying to escape.
I believe that world is called...
..."REALITY"!

I'm living in a delusion.
Where anything is possible.
So let me enjoy my delusion.
Let me have my fun.
Anyway...
...so what that I'm delusional.
Aren't we all?

*"We're living in a world of make-believe
And trying not to let it show
Maybe in that world of make-believe
Heartaches can turn into joy.*

*We're breathing in the smoke of high and low
We're taking up a lot of room
Somewhere in the dark and silent night
Our prayer will be heard, make it soon.*

*So, fly little bird
Up into the clear blue sky
And carry the word
Love's the only reason why, why."*

-*"Living in a World of Make Believe"*
Performed by: The Moody Blues
Written by: Justin Hayward

"The Don"
21.01.2023

I Am NOT Needy!

(NON Sono Bisognoso!)

I Am NOT Needy!
I don't need anyone!

"The Don"
22.01 2023

Lost in a Lost World

(Perso in un Mondo Perduto)

Who am I?
Where am I?
Where is this place?
I don't belong HERE!
I think that...
...I'm lost in a lost world!

Where have I been?
Where am I going?
How did I get here?
How long will I have to be here for?
Because...
...I am lost in a lost world!

"I woke up today, I was crying
Lost in a lost world
'Cause so many people are dying
Lost in a lost world.

Some of them are living an illusion
Bounded by the darkness of their minds
In their eyes it's nation against nation, against nation
With racial pride sad hearts they hide
Thinking only of themselves
They shun the light
They think they're right
Living in their empty shells.

I woke up today, I was crying
Lost in a lost world
'Cause so many people are dying
Lost in a lost world.

Lost in a lost world
(So many people, so many people)
Lost in a lost world'

- "Lost in a Lost World"
Peformed by: The Moody Blues
Written by: Michael Thomas Pinder

"The Don"
24.01.203

The Last Person Standing
(L'ultima Persona in Piedi)

The last person standing writes the *"Story"*.

"The Don"
26.01.2023

You Were Right

(Avevi Ragione)

You were right when you said...
..."You will miss me more than I will miss you!"

"The Don"
28.01.2023

I'm a Spirit Trapped on this Planet

(Sono uno Spirito Intrappolato su Questo Pianeta)

I'm a spirit trapped on this planet...
...just like you!

"The Don"
28.01.2023

(Lastoria)

It's not *"History"*.
It's not *"Herstory"*.
It's *"Thestory"*.

"The Don"
28.01.2023

𝔐𝔶 ℌ𝔬𝔪𝔢 𝔦𝔰 𝔄𝔴𝔞𝔶𝔰 𝔒𝔭𝔢𝔫

(La Mia Casa è Sempre Aperta)

Come on!
Come in!
My home is always open!
My home is your home!
Mia casa e tua casa!

"The Don"
30.01.2023

"da Boyz"

("i Ragazzi")

Are you in the *group*?
Are you *special*?
Are you one of the *"Chosen Ones"*?
Are you one of *"da Boyz"*?

It's a club.
A *"boyz"* club.
No girls allowed!
Are you one of *"da Boyz"*?

They are *intellectuals (or so they think)*!
They are *cultured (or so they think)*!
They are *cool (or so they think)*!
Are you one of *"da Boyz"*?

I was a member of this exclusive club.
I was an honoured *"guest"*!
I NEVER really belonged!
I was NEVER really, one of *"da Boyz"*.

I am no longer one of *"da Boyz"*.
I left the *"Club"*.
I am flying solo.
Because...
...I am no longer one of *"da Boyz"*?

I didn't even like a couple of them!
Ha!

Are you one of *"da Boyz"*?

*"The boys are back in town (the boys are back in town)
I said (the boys are back in town)
(The boys are back in town)."*

-*"The Boys are Back In Town"*-Thin Lizzy

"The Don"
31.01.2023

Do Not Express Yourself

(Non Esprimerti)

Do not say *what you think*.
Do not say *how you feel*.
Do not say *"I LO♥E you"*.
Do not express yourself!

No one really cares.
Everyone is selfish.
In fact, it will be used against you!
So...
...do not express yourself!

People only care about themselves.
They don't really care about you.
They are only interested in what they can get out of you.
So...
...do not express yourself!

You will be *hurt*.
You will be *used*.
You will be *abused*.
You will be *thrown away!*
So...
...do not express yourself!

Do not express yourself!
Oh o oh!

Do not express yourself!
Oh o oh!

Do not express yourself!

"The Don"
01.02.2023

Who the FUCK are You?

(Chi CAZZO Sei?)

Who the FUCK are you?

"The Don"
01.02.2023

Like a Rolling Stone
(Come una Pietra Rotolante)

That's how I roll.
Down this rocky road.
One needs to keep moving on.
One has to keep rolling.
Like a rolling stone.

Roll over the *holes*.
Roll over the *bumps*.
Roll over the *rocks*.
Roll over the *borders*.
Just keep rolling...
...like a rolling stone.

You can never stop *moving*.
You can never stop *struggling*.
You can never stop *rolling*.
Just keep rolling...
...like a rolling stone.

"How does it feel, how does it feel?
To be without a home
Like a complete unknown,
With no direction home,
like a rolling stone."

-*"Like a Rolling Stone"*-Bob Dylan

"The Don"
05.02.2023

Tough Guys Don't Dance

(I Duri non Ballano)

Wanna be a *dude*?
Wanna be *macho*?
Wanna be a *secret agent*?
Wanna be a *gangsta*?
Wanna be a *Mafioso*?
Wanna be a *"Don"*?
Wanna be "*Capo di Capo*"?
Wanna be a *tough guy*?
Just remember...
...tough guys don't dance!

They also don't smile!

And they certainly don't cry!

"You're lookin' for trouble
You came to the right place

If you're lookin' for trouble
Just look right in my face

Because I'm trouble, baby.
Everybody calls me "Mr T"!
Because I'm trouble, baby,
So don't you mess around with me."

-*"Trouble"*
-Performed by: Elvis Presley
Written by: Jerry Leiber/Mike Stoller

"The Don"
03.02.2023

I WISH I WAS YOU

(Vorrei Essere Te)

You're a *free spirit*.
You're *in control*.
You're *powerful*.
You're a *force to be reckoned with*.
You're *invincible*.
You do *whatever the FUCK you want*.
I wish I was you!

You know exactly *what to say*.
You know exactly *what to do*.
You know exactly *how to act*.
You know exactly *what it's all about*.
You know exactly *the situation*.
You know exactly *what you want*.
I wish I was you!

You like to *control*.
You live to *challenge*.
You like to *be adversarial*.
You like to *win*.
That's why...
...*I wish I was you!*

You like to *play*.
You like to *have FUN*.
You like to have *FUN* with...
...*ME!*
You like to *EAT ME*!
I wish I was you!

I admire your *ENERGY*.
I admire your *FORCE*.
I admire your *FOCUS*.
I admire your *ability to not give a shit*.
I admire your *"Chutzpah"*.
I just *admire you!*
I wish I was you!

Maybe someday, I will be like you!
Maybe someday!

"The Don"
02.02.2023

I Am SO SORRY I FUCKED Up Our Friendship

(Mi Dispiace Tanto di aver Rovinato la Nostra Amicizia)

I am *SO SORRY I FUCKED* up our friendship.
I REALLY mean that!
I am so sorry I let you down.
You have taught me what *"TRUE"* friendship is all about.
Thank you!
I can NEVER forget you.
You are a part of me now because of this!

"The Don"
06.02.2023

Killer on the Road

(Assassino sulla Strada)

There's a killer on the road.
He's carrying a very heavy load.
His brain is squirming like a toad.
Is he a *"psychopath"*?
Is he a *"sociopath"*?
Is he *both*?

There's a killer on the road.
He's going to explode.
His brain is going to implode.
Is his *crazy*?
Is he *mad*?
Is he *both*?

There's a killer on the road.
His brain is going to corrode.
His mind is full of mould.
Is he *alive*?
Is he *dead*?
Is he *both*?

There's a killer on the road.
And that killer is *ME*!
Aren't we ALL killers on the road?

"There's a killer on the road
His brain is squirmin' like a toad
Take a long holiday
Let your children play
If you give this man a ride
Sweet family will die
Killer on the road, yeah."

-"Riders on the Storm"-The Doors

"The Don"
08.02 2023

I Don't LO♥E You Anymore
(Non Ti AMO Piu')

I don't LO♥E you anymore!
"NOW we can be friends!"

"It's TOO late!"

"The Don"
08.02.2023

I Bring You LIFE

(Ti Porto la VITA)

I bring you LIFE!
In ALL it's forms.
In ALL it's expressions.
That's what I bring you.
I bring you LIFE!

"The Don"
08.02.2023

Sei Forte

(You are Strong)

Sei *coraggioso*.
Sei *potente*.
Sei *resiliente*.
Sei in *controllo*.
Sei *invincibile*.
Sei *una donna eccezionale*.
Sei forte.

Una vita *senza paura*.
Una vita piena di *sogni*.
Una vita piena di *speranza*.
Una vita piena di *alegria*.
Una vita piena di *risata*.
Una vita piena di *forza*.
Una vita piena di *potere*.
Una vita piena *d'amore*.
Sei forte.

Hai ottanta-quattro anni jovene.
Buon compleanno!

"The Don"
10.02.2023

I DON'T WANT TO LET YOU GO

(Non Voglio Lasciarti Andare)

I don't want to let you go.
We have *unfinished business*.
We have *to be friends before it's over*.
I won't *stop*.
I won't *waver*.
I won't *give up*.
Only until we become friends again will I...
...stop!
I don't want to let you go.

That is my *goal*.
That is my *mission*.
That is my *ending*.
Only until we become friends again will I...
...stop!
I don't want to let you go.

"Don't stop thinking about tomorrow
Don't stop, it'll soon be here
It'll be better than before
Yesterday's gone, yesterday's gone.

Don't stop thinking about tomorrow
Don't stop, it'll soon be here
It'll be better than before
Yesterday's gone, yesterday's gone."

-"Don't Stop"
Performed by: Fleetwood Mac
Written by: Christine McVie

"The Don"
10.02.2023

There is No One!

(Non C'è Nessuno!)

There is no one!
You're ALL alone!
Immerse yourself in the *"Nothing"*.

"The Don"
10.02.2023

No Expectations

(Senza Aspettative)

Do not expect any *calls*.
Do not expect any *contact*.
Do not expect any *kindness*.
Do not expect any *care*.
Do not expect any *compassion*.
Do not expect any *respect*.
Do not expect any *friendship*.
Do not expect any *loyalty*.
Do not expect any *affection*.
Do not expect any *sympathy*.
Do not expect any *empathy*
Do not expect any *fucking*.
And certainly...
...do NOT expect any *LO♥E*!

Do not expect ANYTHING from me!

I don't!

I have NO expectations of you!

"The Don"
13.02 2023

LO♥E in Vain

(Amore in Vano)

Is my LO♥E in vain?
Is your LO♥E in vain?
Is our LO♥E in vain?
Is ALL LO♥E in vain?
Is LO♥E in vain?

"Well, I followed her to the station
With a suitcase in my hand
Yeah, I followed her to the station
With a suitcase in my hand
Whoa, it's hard to tell, it's hard to tell
When all your love's in vain

When the train come in the station
I looked her in the eye
Well, the train come in the station
And I looked her in the eye
Whoa, I felt so sad so lonesome
That I could not help but cry

When the train left the station
It had two lights on behind
Yeah, when the train left the station
It had two lights on behind
Whoa, the blue light was my baby
And the red light was my mind
All my love was in vain.

All my love's in vain."

- *"Love in Vain"*
Written by: Robert Johnson
Performed by: The Rolling Stones

"The Don"
13.02 2023

Sweet Vagina

(Dolce Vagina)

Sweet *"Honey Pot"*.
Sweet *"Pot of Gold.*
Sweet *"Treasure Chest"*.
Sweet *"Fabulous Fanny"*.
Sweet *"Perfumed Pussy"*.
Sweet *"Nectar of the Gods"*.
Sweet *"Cave of Pleasure"*.
Sweet *"Tunnel of LO♥E"*.
Sweet *"Sweet Spot"*.
Sweet *"Glory Hole"*.
Sweet *"LO♥E Hole"*.
Sweet *"Muff Hole"*.
Sweet *"Vagina Monologues"*.
Sweet *"Slitty Slit"*.
Sweet *"Cunning Stunts"*.
Sweet *"Flowery Twats"*
Sweet *"Pussy POWER"*.
Sweet *VAGINA*!

*"Why don't you come on,
Come on down, Sweet Vagina?
Come on, honey child, beg you.
Come on, come on down, you got it in ya.
Got to scrape the shit right off your shoes."*

*-"Sweet Virginia"
Written by: Jagger & Richards
Performed by: The Rolling Stones*

"The Don"
13.02.2023

Don't Chase It

(Non Inseguirlo)

Don't chase it.
It will come to you...
...if it wants to!

Whatever *"It"* is!

"The Don"
13.02.2023

Psychopath or Sociopath?

(Psicopatico o Sociopatico?)

We are ALL CRAAAAAZYYYYYY!
That's a fact!
But which sorta *CRAZY* are you?
Are you a psychopath or a sociopath?

Let me explain the two.
A *psychopath* behaves normal, looks normal, but inside is completely *CRAZY...*
...completely *INSANE*!
He/she just hides it.

A *sociopath* on the other hand doesn't behave normal, doesn't look NORMAL & is obviously completely *CRAZY...*
...completely *INSANE*!
He/she just doesn't hide it at all.

I think I'm a *psychopath*.

What are you?

"I'm going psycho!"

"I said mama we're all crazy now
I said mama we're all crazy now
I said mama we're all crazy now."

-"Mama Weer All Crazee Now"
Performed by: Slade
Written by Neville Holder/James Lea

"The Don"
13.02.2023

My Delusion/Your Reality

(La Mia Illusione/La Tua Realtà)

It's better to live in my *delusion* than...
...in your *reality*!

"The Don"
14.02.2023

NO PRESSURE

(Nessuna Pressione)

No *commitments*.
No *obligations*.
No *assumptions*.
No *expectations*.
No *desires*.
No *longings*.
No *pinings*.
No *yearnings*.
No *lustings*.
No *neediness*.
No *delusions*.
No *illusions*.
No *tricks*.
No *games*.
No *manipulations*.
No *unacceptances*.
No *arguments*.
No *convincing*.
No *coercion*.
No *abuse*.
No *violence*.
No *LO♥E*!

"No PRESSURE!"

"The Don"
15.02.2023

In "Absentia"

(Nella Assenza)

I miss *our talks*.
I miss *talking to you*.
I have to talk to you in *"your absence"*.
I have to talk to you *"In Absentia"*.

"The Don"
15.02.2023

Any LO♥IN' is Good LO♥IN'
(Ogni AMORE è un Buon AMORE)

Any LO♥IN' is good LO♥IN'.
So, take what you can get!

"The Don"
15.02.2023

You're a Fantasist

(Sei un Fantasista)

You *daydream*.
You *romantise*.
You *emotionalise*.
You *theorise*.
You *hypothersise*.
You *extrapolise*.
You *philosophise*.
You *polarise*.
You *fantasise*.

You are a FANTASIST!

By *"You"*, I mean *"Me"*!

"The Don"
17.02.2023

Mr Rejection

(Signore Rifiuto)

I've been rejected so many times it's tattooed on my forehead!

"The Don"
19.02.2023

Do Not Expect Anything

(Non Aspettarti Nulla)

Do not expect anything from me!
We all have *expectations*.
We all have *wants*.
We all have *needs*.
We all have *desires*.
We all have *expectations*.

Even you have expectations.

Expectations are *difficult not to have*.
Expectations are *hard to get rid of*.
Expectations are *dangerous*.
Expectations *cause suffering*.
Do not have any expectations.
So...
...do not expect anything from.

I'll try my best.
But...
...I'll probably fail!

"The Don"
20.02.2023

DON'T BEG FOR LO♥E!

(Non Implorare AMORE!)

Don't Beg For LO♥E!

NEVER, EVER...
...beg for LO♥E!

"The Don"
21.02.2023

Virus

(Virus)

There's a virus that is so stupid it consumes its host...
...in so doing, killing itself.
That virus is called *"Humans"*.
The host is *Earth*.

"The Don"
23.02.2023

State of Mind

(Stato Mentale)

It's ALL a state of mind!

"The Don"
26.02.2023

Paradise

(Paradiso)

Stop…
...wishing & hoping & praying & dreaming & fantasising & imagining.
This is paradise...
...if we want it to be.

"The Don"
28.02.2023

The Stranger

(Lo Sconosciuto)

Who is this figure that walks out of the shadows?
It is wearing a long, black coat with a hood.
I can't make out its face.
Is it a *man*?
Is it a *woman*?
Is it even *human*?
What does it want?
Whom does it seek?
Is it *you*?
Is it *me*?
Can it speak?
Does it even have corporeal form?
Is it an *omen*?
Is it a *sign*?
Is it *"Good"*?
Or...
...is it *"Evil"*?
Is it *"Death"* itself, come to take me away?

Is this my final dance?
Will I be exiting *"stage left"*?
Is this my *final curtain*?
Is this *"The End"*?
Will this be my *final bow*?
Is this when the *"walls come down"*?
Is this my *"swansong"*?

It starts to approach me.
It walks slowly, solemnly.
Methodical & precise.

I am transfixed.
I cannot move.
My body has become numb.
It stretches out its left arm.
I finger touches my left shoulder.
I turn around.
I see a narrow, dimly lit, cobblestone lane.
There is a lamp at the far end.
Beneath is umbra stands a person.

I start to walk.
Moving methodically, precisely, slowly.
The person under the lamp stands transfixed.
As if its body is numb.
I approach it, methodically, precisely, slowly.

"The Don"
28.02.2023

Life Rules

(The Rules of Life)

(Le Regole della Vita)

Don't *talk too much.*
Don't *laugh too much.*
Don't be *funny.*
Don't be a *comedian.*
Don't be *needy.*
Don't be *clingy.*
Don't be *easy.*

Don't have *expectations.*
Don't have *desires.*
Don't express your *emotions.*
Don't express your *feelings.*
Don't be *affectionate.*
Don't *"bend the knee"* (for anyone).
Don't *make any moves.*
Don't *ask for anything.*
Whatever you do...
...DON'T *beg (especially for LO♥E)*
And most importantly...
...NEVER say "I LO♥E you"!

Be *cool.*
Be *silent.*
Be *sullen.*
Be *stoic.*
Be *lofty.*
Be *remote.*
Be *Secretive.*
Be *independent.*
Be *confident.*
Be *resilient.*
Be *"Self-contained".*

Be *spontaneous*.
Be *mysterious*.
Be *elusive*.
Be *enigmatic*.
Be *unattainable*.
Be an *"Observer"*.
Be *in control*.
Be a *listener*

"WTF..."
"...there are too many FUCKING rules!"
"Life is complicated!"

"The Don"
28.02.2023

By the Rivers of Babylon

(Presso i Fiumi di Babilonia)

Take me back to *Mesopotamia*.
Take me back to *Nineveh*.
The *"Cradle of Civilisation"*.
The land between the two mighty rivers...
...the *Tigres* & the *Euphrates*.
Where the great *"Gilgamesh"* once ruled.
That is my home.
That is where I was born.
That is where I'll die.

I have *existed for six thousand years*.
I have *seen everything*.
I have *been a witness to everything*.
I have *created everything*.
I can destroy everything.

I *know all the old knowledge*.
I have *written all the old stories*.
I have *created all the "Gods"*.
I have *lived in "Hell"*.
I have seen *once great cities turn into sand*.
I have seen *death & destruction of worlds*.
Destroyed by greed & arrogance.
But I did not die.
I still exist.

I am *inside you*.
I am *inside everything*.
I am *everywhere*.
I cannot *die*.
I cannot be *killed*.
I cannot be *destroyed*.
I *will never die*.
Because I know the secret of immortality.

If you want to find me...
...you know where I am.

"By the rivers of Babylon, there we sat down.
Yeah, we wept, when we remembered Sargon.
By the rivers of Babylon, there we sat down.
Yeah, we wept, when we remembered Sargon."

-"Rivers of Babylon"
Performed by: Boney M
Written by: Dowe/Farian/Reyam/McNaughton

"Dedicated to my friend, Sonny"

"The Don"
28.02.2023

Can We Start Again?

(Possiamo Ricominciare?)

Can we *go back to the beginning?*
Can we *erase the past?*
Can we start all over again?
Can we *forget everything up to this point?*
Can we *start afresh?*
Can we *forget what's happened?*
Can we *forget all my mistakes?*
Can we *forgive my stupidity?*
Can we start again?

Is that possible?

I'd like that!

"The Don"
02.03.2023

(Epifania)

Enlightenment.
Clarity.
Certainty.
Profundity.

A *mysterious experience.*
A *magical experience.*
A *spiritual experience.*
A *"Religious" experience.*
A *"Holy" experience.*

An *awakening.*
A *realization.*
An *orgasm.*

"She ain't NEVER going to have an Epiphany!"

"The Don"
03.03.2023

In the Garden of Eden

(Nel Giardino dell'Eden)

That's where it all started.
In the "Garden of Eden".
Our first sin.
In the "Garden of Eden".
"Original Sin".
In the "Garden of Eden".
When Adam was seduced by the Devil.
In the "Garden of Eden".
"Take this delicious apple", he said.
In the "Garden of Eden".
"Take it to Eve".
In the "Garden of Eden".
"*She'll like it*".
In the "Garden of Eden".
"She will never have tasted anything like this before", he continued.
In the "Garden of Eden".
"It is so sweet. Its nectar is like honey from God.".
In the "Garden of Eden".
Adam took the apple.
In the "Garden of Eden".
Convinced by the Devil's words.
In the "Garden of Eden".
He handed it to Eve.
In the "Garden of Eden".
"Taste this apple", he said.
In the "Garden of Eden".
"Have a bite".
In the "Garden of Eden".
"It is supposed tastes so sweet, like the nectar of God", said Adam.
In the "Garden of Eden".
Eve took a bite.
In the "Garden of Eden".
She felt is sweetness in her mouth.
In the "Garden of Eden".
It truly did taste like the nectar of God!
In the "Garden of Eden".

"In the garden of Eden, honey
Don't you know that I'm lovin' you

In a gadda da vida, baby
Don't you know that I'll always be true.

In a gadda da vida, honey
A garden just meant for two.

In a gadda da vida, baby
A garden only for me & you.

In a gadda da vida, honey
Don't you know that I'll always be true.

Oh, won't you come with me.
And take my hand.
Oh, won't you come with me
And walk this land
Please take my hand.

In a gadda da vida, honey.
Don't you know that I'm lovin' you.
In a gadda da vida, baby
Don't you know that I'll always be true

Oh, won't you come with me
And take my hand
Oh, won't you come with me
And walk this land
Please take my hand."

-"In-A-Gadda-Da-Vida"
Performed by: Iron Butterfly
Written by: Douglas Ingle

"The Don"
03.03.2023

Books written by "The Don"

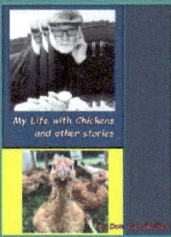

"My Life with Chickens & other stories: I Pity the Poor Immigrant"
Published:
10th September, 2019
Autobiography Book 1:
0 – 12 years old

"Poems for Misfits, Miscreants, Misanthropes, Mavericks, Losers & Malcontents!"
Published:
10th June, 2020
Book of Poems 1

"Poems for Troubled Minds & Trouble Hearts"
Published:
10th August, 2020

Book of Poems 2

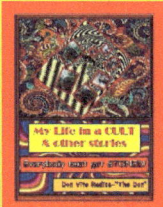

"My Life in a CULT & other stories: Everybody Must Get STONED!"
Published:
10th September, 2020
Autobiography Book 2:
15 – 30 years old

"Poems for Restless Minds & Restless Hearts"
Published:
10th October, 2020
Book of Poems 3

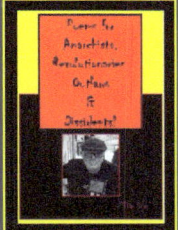

"Poems for Anarchists, Revolutionaries, Outlaws & Dissidents!"
Published:
10th November, 2020

Book of Poems 4

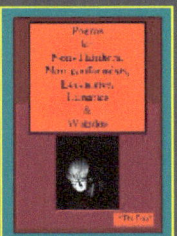

"Poems for Non-Thinkers & Eccentrics"
Published:
10th December, 2020
Book of Poems 5

"The Rantings of a Madman"
Published:
10th January, 2021

Book of Poems 6

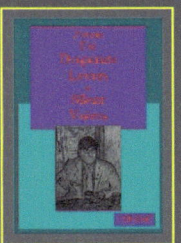

"Poems for Desperate Lovers & Silent Voices"
Published:
10th February, 2021
Book of Poems 7

"Poems for Tormented Minds & Tortured Souls"
Published:
10th March, 2021
Book of Poems 8

All available ONLY online

Books written by "The Don"

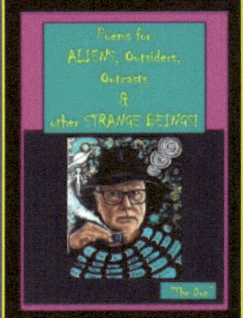

"Poems for ALIENS, Outsiders, Outcasts & other STRANGE BEINGS!"
Published: 10th April, 2021
Book of Poems 9

"Poems for Beings From Another Planet"
Published: 10th May, 2021
Book of Poems 10

"Poems for Mindless Beings & Lost Souls"
Published: 10th June, 2021
Book of Poems 11

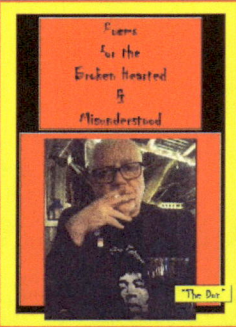

"Poems for the Broken Hearted & Misunderstood
Published: 10th July, 2021
Book of Poems 12

"Poems for Poems for the Bewildered, Dazed & Confused"
10th August, 2021
Book of Poems 13

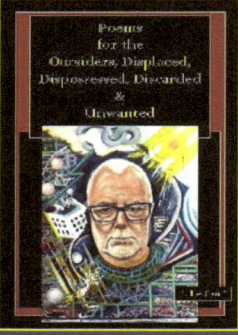

"Poems for the Outsiders, Displaced, Dispossessed, Discarded & Unwanted"
Published: 10th Sept, 2021
Book of Poems 14

All available ONLY online

"Poems for Secret Agents, Phantom Agents, Agents of Change, Agent Provocateurs & Agents of Chaos"
Published: 10th Oct, 2021
Book of Poems 15

"Poems for Disenchanted, Disillusioned & Delusional"
Published: 10th November, 2021
Book of Poems 16

Books written by "The Don"

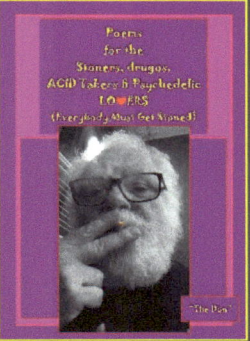

"Poems for the Stoners, drugos, ACID takers & Psychedelic LO♥ERS (Everybody Must Get Stoned)"
Published: 10th December, 2021
Book of Poems 17

"Poems for Anarchists, Rebels & Revolutionaries
Published: 10th January, 2022
Book of Poems 18

"Poems for Rebels, Radicals & Revolutionaries (Viva la Révolution!)"
Published: 10th February, 2022
Book of Poems 19

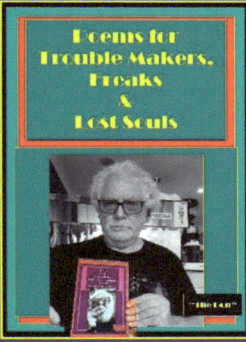

"Poems for Trouble Makers, Freaks & Lost Souls"
Published: 10th March 2022
Book of Poems 20

"Poems for Zombies & the Walking Dead"
Published: 10th April 2022
Book of Poems 21

"Poems for Non-Conformists (Never conform!)"
Published: 10th May 2022
Book of Poems 22

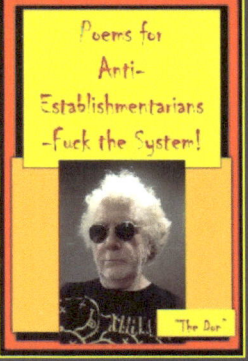

"Poems for Anti-Establishmentarians -Fuck the System!"
Published: 10th June 2022
Book of Poems 23

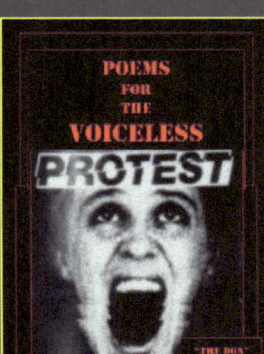

"Poems for the Voiceless"
Published: 10th July 2022
Book of Poems 24

All available ONLY online

Books written by "The Don"

"Poems for the Fearless"

Published: 10th August 2022

Book of Poems 25

"Poems for the PEACEMAKER: Make peace NOT war!"

Published: 10th March 2023

Book of Poems 26

"Poems for the Forever Young (May you stay forever young!)
Published:
10th June 2023
Book of Poems 27

"Poems for the Children of the REVOLUTION!
Published:
10th October 2023

Book of Poems 28

All available ONLY

www.ingramcontent.com/pod-product-compliance
Lightning Source LLC
Chambersburg PA
CBHW041502010526
44107CB00049B/1629